Mother Natured

Poems and Images of Presence, Wonder, and Gratitude

Brienne Sembrat

For Mom, Aunt Lynne,
Aunt Happy, and Aunt Elsa Jane.

Spreading love with gardens.

© 2025, Brienne Sembrat.

All rights reserved. This book or any portion thereof may not be reproduced or used in any manner whatsoever without the express written permission of the publisher except for the use of brief quotations in a book review.
ISBN: 979-8-35099-443-8 (hard cover)

Contents

Unplugged	1

SPRING 3

Memory of Hyacinth	5
Windflower	7
Magnolia Mindset	9
Snapshot	11
Sweet Lilac	13
Small Wonders	15
Whisper Tread	17
Stay	19
True	21

SUMMER 23

First Days of June	25
Wise Elder	27
New Trail	29
Shore Natured	31
The Chicory and the Bee	33
Green Gratitude	35
High Hydrangea	37
Pond Reflections	39
Hemlock	41
Summer Saunter	43
Gra-tree-tude	45
Sunflower Days	47
Summer's Turn	49
Journey	51

AUTUMN 53

Closer	55
September Field	57
Season's Meeting	59
Autumn Tale	61
Autumn Rose	63
Autumn Home	65
November Field	67
The Milkweed and the Monarch	69
Rest	71

WINTER 73

Winter's Dance	75
Winter Wanderer	77
Winter's Ways	79
Hellebore	81
January	83
Winter's Shape	85
The Sky Today	87
Daffodil	89
Harbinger	91
Snowdrop Morning	93
Mother Natured	95

Unplugged

The unplugged world she calls to me:
wind, birds, leaves, trees.
My home has walls, yet just a thin veil,
so dirt itself can be my trail.
If not the woods, then yard or park:
blue sky, sun warm, drizzle, or dark.
My feet on paths, my mind reframes,
the swirling thoughts my senses tame.
I walk, play, dig, or merely be
as nature's pace revises me.
Earth will ease us, we are bound,
together life can be refound.

Spring

Memory of Hyacinth

Saddle shoe, rock garden stair,
a chilly sun, wind-blown kid hair.
It's early morn in hopeful May,
the bright green grass, a place to play.
Near Crocus bright she gathers round,
just one small girl, keen eyes to ground.
'Neath snow white blooms from the Apple tree,
no fear of earth or muddy knees,
she crouches down, dips nose to stem
for Hyacinth does bloom again.
And in that scent, blue-violet mist,
does spring alight and winter list.
Now skip away to meet the day!
Your natured heart is here to stay.

Windflower

Dark gray eve in early spring,
trees' yet-furled leaves, few flowering.
But the air is soft; sweet breezes blow,
I look to the sky and earth below.
Life incubates, so spring heart waits;
these slower steps a seeker's gait.
On mounding copse, my eye does spy,
gath'ring of blooms just ankle high.
A hue so sweet, blue-purple light,
as Windflowers sing to soothe the night.

Magnolia Mindset

Natured folk fear not at all
that new day's bloom may next day fall
to cold in March's ephemeral way,
one day of sun, one day of gray.
For ice can bite or snow can lay,
the petals brown and buds decay.
But stop instead and pause to know,
these magic blooms that thrive and grow
in bright pink Lotus-like display,
none match her sweet, lovely array.
So breathe and be and look to sky,
Magnolia bright is here and nigh,
and let not knowing be alright,
for present moments hold the light.

Snapshot

As Tulips stretch to sun and light,
the rays a gild to petals bright,
I'll keep the picture in mind's sight,
a lift on darker days.
Just as the bulb tucks under the earth,
awaiting spring and bloom's rebirth,
the stretch to come, a treasure's worth,
of hope and nature's ways.

Sweet Lilac

A late Sunday walk

and sweet April's soon spent.

Purple Lilac blooms call

on air heavy with scent.

Kwanzan Cherries sing pink,

while the Dogwoods trill white,

as the golden sun croons

into blue and green night.

I will lay down my head,

dreaming songs of Earth's spring,

hues that chorus with joy,

resonate, and take wing.

Small Wonders

When we slow down
in nature's land,
the very small
becomes quite grand.
Each tiny being
a beauty be,
each little sprout
we bow to see.
A mountaintop
or spring-valley new,
such spreads of scope
we love to view.
But in the breach
of root and rill,
much wonder lies
in one small Squill.

Whisper Tread

I took a walk
to smell the air,
to rest my thoughts,
lay down my cares.
My mind was caught,
but feet, they trod,
found dirt and trees
as blooming sought.
I heard the rill,
heart set to thrill,

I gently crept
just down the hill.
And there it was,
a magic spot,
a flower's glow,
a water's drop.
And now each day
my whisper tread
follows my heart
to rest my head.

Stay

Seek we not to look away

from tree bright blooms that had their day,

for petals down mean leaves aloft,

a summer's breeze, a fall so soft.

Each day is new, and so might we

watch each small step all nature see.

True

When I choose
to take a stroll
I find myself
the more to know.
The natured land
minds not the skin,
minds not what's grand
or where I've been.
But only seeks
to be herself,
no thought to things,
no thought to wealth.
Just grows and thrives,
seeks water, light,
helps neighbors grow,
a welcome sight.
Thus nature is
by truth alone
a precious land
we call our home.

Summer

First Days of June

First days of June

the light streams high

cross mountains, creek,

and azure sky.

By lakeside rock

and trailside green

minders may slow

to know the scene.

Daisies make way,

bright glows each one.

We lift our heads

with joy for sun.

Wise Elder

Can we slow down
enough to see
Box Elder seeds
amid the sway
of blooms so fine
they hold our gaze
but rain and sun
have many ways.
And if we pause,
slow each footfall,
we may just spot
the best of all.

New Trail

The way of spring
was fresh and green,
the trail was wide
my feet to guide.
I walked and smiled
at once beguiled,
the verge so soft
more tame than wild.
Then summer's breath
brought growth and spread,
trail-blanket strewn
by flora's bed.
So seek will I
new land and sky,
perhaps cool mountains
now to try.
And then next spring
right after snow,
return once more
where wildflowers grow.

Shore Natured

I meet the sea
and breathe in slow,
where waves push sand
and breezes blow.
The Sea Oats bow,
the Gulls take flight,
skin-coat of salt,
eyes filled with light.
Then wander in
where sound meets land,
Crepe Myrtles teem,
pink blossoms grand.

The birds, the shells,
sea glass aglow,
as ocean beats,
my heart in flow.
Sunbeaten wood,
a sailboat's wing,
house made of books,
a gray porch swing.
The clouds may build,
a sun may set,
a heart may stay,
not soon forget.

The Chicory and the Bee

A life on the wing,

a busy big bee,

much work to be done

on flower and tree.

What perch prefer?

A bloom you seek most?

Where pollen is best

or color your host?

If I were a bee,

and if I could choose,

I'd pick Chicory

for the magical blues.

Green Gratitude

As I walk, I clear my mind
and watch the dirt beneath my feet.
I see the stems of lit green hues
and blooms of colors spilling out.
I breathe sweet air that reaches down
to fill my lungs and wrap my heart.
The breeze, so light upon my skin,
a nudge of wind that cools and soothes.
The sun, so bright it lingers low,
promise of heat but cool for now.
My thoughts stay close and blessedly
my calm breath keeps me clear and free.
A morning walk to start my day
with gratitude for the green array.

High Hydrangea

Soft colors meld,

my eye is held,

a breath to calm,

'tis nature's balm.

What color thy?

Not land or sky:

pink, yellow, blue,

an ethereal hue.

A leaf so bright

in evening light

and barnwood gray

backdrops array.

I can't but think

this heavenly blush

is but a stroke

of greatest brush.

Pond Reflections

Serene as eve

but bright the day,

top water's peace

cool colors lay.

Upon the land

the air is light,

reflections true

capture the hue.

A lovely pond,

my heart grows fond,

concerns console,

and ease the soul.

Hemlock

A tiny tree from old one's fell,

the log now gives a growing spell.

While moss and fungi help to bring

what saplings need from the earth to spring

from beds of love in rooms of green,

as light pours through the verdant screen.

Such years, wisdom, strength, scale,

weave ancient giant Hemlock's tale.

Summer Saunter

Slow steps and pause for garden view,
sun-lit petal, morning dew.
Color o'er a rainbow's arch,
not red or orange, a higher hue.
White picket fence and blue, blue sky,
tall trees that stretch to clouds on high.
A quiet road, a bright green leaf,
a Rose, a walk, a natured sigh.

Gra-tree-tude

A walk through town
in steamy July,
and sun pours rays
from hazy blue skies.
Cement and bricks crack
from heat and duress,
no fever cure here,
no refuge possess.
Leave blacktop behind
for a cool, verdant space,
as deep green boughs will shade
a sweat-beaded face.
Moss, creek, and dirt soothe
like a balm for the feet,
so the trees I will thank
for shadows so sweet.
A forest knows how,
in wise and old ways,
to perfect the air,
make temperate the days.

Sunflower Days

When the sky is bright blue,
angled light warms the fields.
When some blooms become few,
August crop's final yield.
In the heat's waning hours,
autumn signs may now show,
then look up to Sunflower,
summer's joy you will know.

Summer's Turn

Late August heat and cloudless day,

grass blades turn brown, some buds decay.

Growth slows, leaves fade, summer's decline,

the sun seeks not such lofty line.

As nature tires, the pace may slow,

spring's bright green burst to memory go.

Yet not all fade in dusty beds,

on garden's edge, the Tea Rose spreads.

Her glow of second bloom, a light,

a beacon now, a message bright

that floras come and seasons go,

a time to rest, a time to grow.

Some favored now, others will wait,

for earth to turn, new chance, new fate.

Next August may a rain dance be

so rose to succumb to moldy spree.

And other blooms can last dance twirl

while autumn waits, and Oak leaves furl.

Journey

I used to hike and pound the trail,
my counted steps felt golden.
Must reach the end, the peak, the top,
to end line was beholden.
This way I loved,
the trail drew me,
the dappled light, the fun.
I did not know at this time past,
that land and I were one.
So quick I flew,
I talked and climbed,
I won't forget these hours.
But now I see I only sensed
a bit of nature's powers.
I sought the woods,
I knew not why;
I felt alive,
the rocks, the sky.
But maybe just a passerby?
I saunter now with gentle feet,
the earth herself with peace I greet.
My reverence soft and senses wide,
gently cued to all I find.
I move quite slow, my breath I set,
with mindfulness I place each step.
Disturbed by me I will not let,
and then my senses free mind's net.
Hard thoughts can drop,
soft peace can rise,
I may just lay and view the skies.
There is no goal to put in place,
but greet the land and thank the grace,
to know what's here and truly bind,
as nature heals this modern mind.

Autumn

Closer

September now
brings cooler air,
the gardens show
less hue and care.
Sun changes theme,
the squirrels prepare,
scoop Acorn nuts
lest food is spare.
On woods and mottes
tinged leaf, fall's kiss,
but Sharon's Rose
holds summer's bliss.

As blooms began
some months ago,
now change of heart
does nature know.
Our harvest time
lies nearer then
when bud and sprout
and life began.
So when I gaze
on white rose glow,
see not Snowdrop,
remember snow.

September Field

Days hot and light,

but cool the night,

to autumn field

my heart does yield.

As meadows roll

the sight guides the soul

to Goldenrod,

grass gently plod.

The Lace of Queens

and Iron Beams,

a purple deep,

not yet to sleep.

And winged one land

on blooming hand,

for bees still roam

late summer's home.

Season's Meeting

When late summer warmth
meets autumn's sweet ways,
when the sky's bluey blue
forms a cool canvas glaze.
Then two seasons may blend
for the best of earth's show,
leaf edges are bright
but the berries still glow.
It is almost too much
for just one heart to hold;
a land of such grace
is more treasure than gold.
We walk softly then,
slow a bit, heed her call,
for the nature-made brush
paints the best art of all.

Autumn Tale

Once upon autumn,
in the east of the land,
in the north of the hills,
where the changes are grand,
where the natured ones twirl
'neath the bright boughs of fall,
singing season's sweet song,
sprinkling wonder on all.
Maples glow ruby red,
dragon Oak's copper fire,
giant Beeches drip gold,
to deep wonder inspire.
Pine still wears hunter's green,
courting plummy-clad Pear,
shod by underbrush bright,
what will young Sweetgum wear?
A queen's treasure lies here,
stately guards, handsome trees,
minding kingdoms of hue,
bard birds sing, knights bend knees.
Like a fantasy tale,
richly patterned and spun,
so the maker's loom weaves
tapestries lit by the sun.
Em'rald grass carpets all,
'neath the tent's dreamy blue,
with the colors between,
what's the reader to do?
We might linger and still
ponder life, breathe in true
parchment leaf earthy scents,
magic words, glamoured view.
Feel deep wellspring of heart
at the journey's last page,
for such splendor is real,
love the book, thank the sage!

Autumn Rose

The last of the blooms
to catch the seeker's eye,
raindrops and a chill
'neath late autumn's gray sky.
One bright Rose holds on,
whose color we know,
through winter white way,
the heart holds close such glow.
Then spring warms the ice,
green stem bursts old leaf,
so summer plant grows
with bud underneath.
Then bright fall paints again,
to return blossoms live.
In an earth-tended soul,
Nature's hues always thrive.

Autumn Home

Stop and look up
to see autumn's home,
fantastical place,
this high-natured space.
May long to climb in
and see from within,
chair made of hardwood,
hearth lit by a sunbeam,
walls painted in leaf,
eyes soothed by what's real.
I'll stay and just be,
tucked in the fall tree.

November Field

November field

and sun is low,

where colors are soft

and leaves fall slow.

The Goldenrod

has lost her glow,

yet eyes find joy

in texture's show.

On flaxen stems

winged seeds now be,

catch light and wind,

fall fields and me.

The Milkweed and the Monarch

The Monarch flew
some months ago
to warmer climes,
new life to know.
But low and cool
is northern light,
soft blue and brown
to soothe the sight.
On waning stems
in evening glow,
the Milkweed seeds
are set to go.

Just smooth as silk
the pips have wings,
to find new homes,
spring growth to bring.
On coats of Deer
or wind's strong hand,
they'll move to find
a place to land.
And then in June,
when sun is high,
such a joyful boon!
the Monarchs fly.

Rest

A spent summer bud
backlit by low light,
a different view now,
no pink Rosebud bright,
no leafy green keep,
just empty cracked shell,
a hard-sleeping branch,
"winter comes," all do tell.
But my eye has changed too
as I shift with the time,
this wonder not new,
my state more sublime.

Stark shapes of the land,
what once held the verge,
for the flower we loved
with gray landscape now merge.
And I wonder anew
as the story unfolds,
for in season's contrast
there is value, such gold.
So we welcome dim light
and the branch that bends low,
as deep under and in
all can rest, soon to grow.

Winter

Winter's Dance

A graceful dry bloom
in December's cold room,
bend close to know
how life once did grow.
All petals don veins
that moved drops of rain
to lift what was new
when warm sun leapt through.
The old too is fine,
held still, keeping time.
Spent bloom I'll hold dear
as snowflakes swirl near.
She may crumble now,
if wet snow, she'll bow.
Each note has to play,
wintertide, nature's sway.

Winter Wanderer

The trees were so bare yet in cold they stood strong;
'twas the wind and dry beech leaves that held nature's song.
The Oak said to me, "This is not our time,
we are slumbering now, our beauty sublime."
The Maple reached up sky-high to the blue,
and said to the heights, "This time is for you."
Sycamore roots reached to river below,
"Bring the reflections while we wait to grow."
The Hickory leaned toward his friend, the pine,
"Neighbor, I'll rest, but it's your time to shine."
As the Earth spins, makes her way 'round the sun,
nature's beauty and awe after fall are not done.
The eye may note blue, and the eye may note brown,
but twixt heavens and creek, there is pine with snow gown.
For the sky and the water and the Firs guide the way.
I love winter woods, for there's always display.

Winter's Ways

The green life rests,
the fauna trucks in,
the snow lays a blanket
to hush the world's din.
The cold winds, they test,
and harsh are some days,
a value in contrast
to spring's warming ways.
Flora colors are muted,
sunset skies light the eve,
on snow's open canvas
stark shadows do weave.
Nature, you slumber,
and spring draws so near,
yet winter gives much
to hold near and dear.

Hellebore

A break in the chill,
midwinter's warm sigh,
rivulet of snowmelt
and sunshine is nigh.
So most flora sleeps on
for this day shall not hold,
chill breath will return
gray skies and earth cold.
But like water that runs
as an icicle melts,
so the Hellebore never
stops being herself.
As not only with blooms
but in buds she'll display
winter beauty indeed,
deep strength, nature's way.
And she'll dance in the snow
and she'll sing in the night,
for her spirit grows high
when the earth dresses white.

January

One month into winter's time
a young year ponders slow,
what will thrive, and what will be,
and what to memory go.
Frigid eve is long and deep,
all waters halt their run,
now time to contemplate and sleep,
our festivals are done.
North people mind the season,
align with light and snow,
one candle's glow is all we need
when sun is angled low.

A Groundhog burrows deep and long,
a Rose bush beauty rest,
so too shall I adjust my step
for nature's pace is best.
Our outside trail may shorten,
as inside nurture bring,
the hygge way is timely,
to read, or cook, or sing.
In January's natured ways
we bless long nights
and thank short days,
mind seeds and rest for spring.

Winter's Shape

The poets write of winter's bones,
the stark shapes made by land and tree,
this sunrise tome of Oak and sky,
a branching black calligraphy.
Spring's thaw and growth are months now gone,
the summer's verge was not to last,
fall's leafy ground now cold and pressed,
the bones of earth exposed, hold fast.
An icy steel from rock and stream,
the forest floor hard packed and still,
boughs frozen pose, sustained with strength,
for held in all is Nature's will.
To stand and stay through every sky,
to guard the inner life, to know
an infrastructure drafted well,
for weighty life that May will grow.

The Sky Today

A moment's pause,
a stop to be,
I rest in awe at
what's over me.
Just bluest sky
on winter's day
can feed a soul
this basic way.
A great beyond
of azure hue,
a wondrous gift
for me and you.

Daffodil

Tuck your heads beneath once more;
this warming spell was not the door
of spring and sun for which you ken,
and will indeed come again.
But snow and ice more moons have we,
so tuck your heads or merely be,
for strength is yours, you will endure,
oh, Daffodil, bright blooms you store!

Harbinger

I sit in this place, at home in my nook,

and quiet my mind with the breath that I tend.

I still racing thoughts by sensing the land,

the seasons they shift, a change is at hand.

I see brighter light.

I hear varied songs.

The earth becomes free.

This home calls to me.

I walk slow with care, or sit still like stone,

and can't help but smile to know what will come.

I met winter well; it held my deep sleep,

now miracles wait, soul gifts I will keep.

Snowdrop Morning

Cold, yet soft,

the snow still lays

upon the earth

'neath winter's gaze.

But not the only white I've found

for Snowdrop peaks above the ground.

Shy yet forthright,

day blooms from night,

the sun spreads warmth,

and light explains

that seasons move,

some nature sleeps,

yet Snowdrop thrives

when cold still reigns.

Mother Natured

A lovely soul did camp with me,
she showed me leaf and bud and tree.
We sang and slept 'neath stars and moon:
the fire, the tale, the earth, the tune.
Now grown 'tis I the camper be,
I set the tent beside the tree.
I hike and sit by falls and rill,
forever grateful for the skill.
But more for love, a grateful me,
for natured mother now I see
I cannot live without the place
where wild ones grow, and I feel grace.

www.hikergirlarts.com